CAN YOU DIG IT?

ARCHAEOLOGY LOST & FOUND
IN THE SANDS OF TIME

AMANDA BAKER

2nd Edition printed 2018

Copyright © 2018, 2017 Amanda Baker

ISBN: 978-1-7307-8806-2

 Published by Panda Archaeology

www.pandaarchaeology.com

For my Grandma, who told
me I should.

There are many people who have helped make this book possible, and, without whom, this would not have happened. Diana Wilde, who has been there with me from the start of this book: thank you for believing bigger than I ever could. Mom & Dad, I cannot express how much I appreciate your support in everything I do! To my siblings, Jessi, Michelle, Nick, Kristin, and Alison, for putting up with my utter geek, and for listening to all of my blabbering about archaeology since we were little. To my grandparents, all of whom have shown me what it means to work hard for what is important in life. Tarece, thank you for always supporting my dream.

I would also like to thank my archaeology friends, teachers, professors, excavation buddies, and editors, who gave me important insights while supporting this journey.

A VERY special thanks goes out to my AMAZING Launch Team, who have helped me make this book the best it can be: AG Morgan, Aimee Oczkowski, Alison Benedict, Brad McKay, Brian Page, Cathy Beck, Charlotte Bregulla, Diana Wilde, Gerald Walling, Jack Connor, Jenn Kinzel, Jenni Julander, Jennifer Dunne, Jessica Baker, JoAnn Baker, Johnny Wang, Kathy Heshelow, Kathy Page, Katy Crofts, Kristin Baker, Laura Baker, Laura Pekkalainen, Lissa Landis, Louise van Niekirk, Mansa Christian, Markus Hochholdinger, Melody Barker, Michelle Baker, Mike Baker, Morgan Perez, Myra Skelton, Nick Baker, Otakara Klettke, Pam Coville, Paresh Patel, Scott Allan, Shannon King, Shelby Ingram, Sheri Farley, Sophie Pickett Russell, Stacy-Ann Moyce-Scruggs, Tara Jayne Schnetz, Tarece Johnson, and Thushani Jayawardena.

I would like to give a special shout out to Chandler Bolt and the Self-Publishing School, who taught me and provided the guidance and support system I needed to actually do this!

Key Terms

Archaeologists: scientists who study archaeology

Archaeology: the science that deals with past human life as shown by fossil relics and the monuments and tools left by ancient peoples

Artifacts (artefacts): a usually simple object (as a tool or ornament) showing human work and representing a culture or a stage in the development of a culture

*artefact and artifact are each acceptable spellings of the same thing.

Bedrock: the solid rock lying under surface materials (as soil) that are not in layers

Context: events in time which have been preserved in the archaeological record. The cutting of a pit or ditch in the past is a context, and the material filling it will be another.

Continuously: continuing without a stop

Deceased: no longer living

Excavation: to expose to view by digging away a covering

Field of study: the particular focus of research

Geologic processes: a natural process whereby geological features are modified

Horizontal: parallel to the horizon

Hunter-gatherer: a member of a culture in which food is gotten by hunting, fishing, and gathering rather than by agriculture

Hypothesis: something not proved but assumed to be true for purposes of argument or further study or investigation

Isotope analysis: the measurement of the ratio of stable and radioactive isotopes of particular elements within chemical compounds. A wide range of archaeological materials such as metals, glass and lead-based pigments have been sourced using isotopic characterization.

Landscape Archaeology: the study of the ways in which people in the past constructed and used the environment around them

Layers of human occupation: stratigraphic layers that show evidence that people lived at a site

Lithic: stone

Open context: excavation strategy where a large area is excavated one context at a time

Osteoarchaeology: the branch of archaeology that deals with the study of bones found at archaeological sites

Paleolithic: of, relating to, or being the earliest period of the Stone Age marked by rough or crudely chipped stone implements. It extends from the earliest known use of stone tools, probably by Homo habilis initially, 2.6 million years ago, to the end of the Pleistocene around 10,000 years before present.

Pits: small units of excavation; alternately, the name of a stratigraphic context cut into a stratum

Pottery sherd: a sherd, or more precisely, potsherd, is commonly a historic or prehistoric fragment of pottery, although the term is occasionally used to refer to fragments of stone and glass vessels, as well

Ritual: an action done in exactly the same way whenever a particular situation occurs; often refers to, but is not exclusive to, religious action

Scientific method: the rules and procedures for the pursuit of knowledge involving the finding and stating of a problem, the collection of facts through observation and experiment, and the making and testing of ideas that need to be proven right or wrong

Settlement: a place where people have come to live and have built homes

Site plan: drawn record of features and artefacts in the horizontal plane

Specialty: an area of archaeology that is of greatest interest to an archaeologist, and is therefore where they focus their research

Stains: Soil that is colored differently from the surrounding context due to a change in human activity (like a pit being refilled, or a leftover post from a structure)

Stratigraphic sequence: the complete record of strata or contexts layered one on top of the other, with the oldest stratum at the bottom, above the bedrock, and the most recently formed stratum at the top of the sequence

Stratigraphy: layers of sedimentation and human occupation events that can be seen through archaeological excavation

Stratum (pl. strata): single layer of soil with internally consistent characteristics (such as color and consistency) that represents a period of human occupation. A stratum is the fundamental unit in a stratigraphic sequence

Vertical: going straight up or down from a level surface

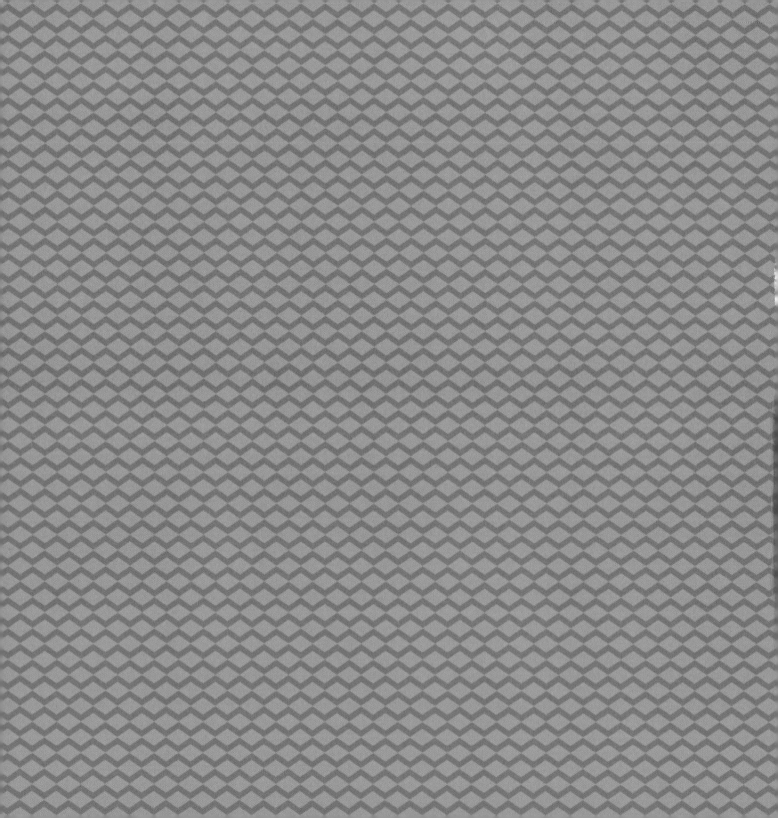

What is archaeology? It is the science of studying past human life through what they left behind, like buildings, tools, and other activities.

Hi! My name is Amanda, and I am an **archaeologist**!

"What is **archaeology**?" you ask? Well, archaeology is the science that studies our human past, and archaeologists are the people who study that past! Archaeologists are probably best known for digging ancient cities out of the ground, but we do so much more than that! We study sites using the scientific method to conduct excavations, test **hypotheses**, and answer questions about people who lived long ago, or not so long ago.

What do Archaeologists Study?

Modern archaeologists are not treasure hunters who go out and search for gold and jewels all the time. In fact, while it is really exciting to find such items, they are rare at most sites. Archaeologists are scientists, and we use the scientific method to gather information that is important for us to understand how a specific group of people used to live.

While archaeologists are often portrayed in movies or television as knowing a lot about many cultures across time and space, the truth is that we tend to focus on a field or a specialty. A field of study is the culture, time period, geographic location, or specialty in which an archaeologist focuses the majority of his/her research.

For example, my field of study is the Bronze Age Mediterranean. I study the cultures surrounding the Mediterranean Sea from about 3500-1200 BCE. Other archaeologists research the prehistoric cultures of the Americas, or the Paleolithic people of Southeast Asia, or Medieval Europe, or even World War II.

Hundreds of these Moai were left behind by the ancient Rapa Nui people on Easter Island.

3

Sphynx, Giza, Egypt

Temple of Quetzalcoatl,
Mexico (replica)

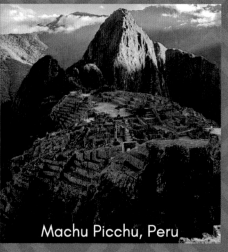
Machu Picchu, Peru

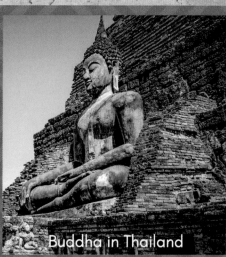
Buddha in Thailand

4

Some archaeologists focus on a particular type of study, and not a culture. For example, a significant trend in archaeology right now is called Landscape Archaeology, where archaeologists try to understand how ancient people interacted with the landscape surrounding them.

Most people would have lived close to water and food sources, the necessities of life. If they were hunter-gatherers who moved around to follow food, they would stay at a site for a short time and would need easy access to shelter and a view of the animal herds they followed. Farming communities need access to good farming land, water (either rain or nearby fresh water sources), and materials for constructing more permanent homes.

Was a settlement built on the highest point in a landscape? Then there is a good chance it was placed there to view all the lands its people controlled or to protect itself from outside invaders.

Ancient Romans would fill the Colosseum with water to recreate naval battles!

Colosseum, Rome, Italy

Artifact specialists are archaeologists who focus their research on a particular type of artifact, such as stone tools, pottery, or bones.

The earliest stone tools date back 3.3 million years ago and change over time. Skilled archaeologists can reproduce various types of stone tools.

Pottery specialists can analyze where pottery was made, where the specific styles originate from, and how the types of pottery used changed over time.

Osteoarchaeologists study bones found at archaeological sites. They look at animal or human bones to figure out the age at death, if there had been any injury during life, and even if that person had certain diseases.

These are just a few specialties that archaeologists can study.

One of the ways we collect information is through an **excavation**. During an excavation, archaeologists carefully dig layers of dirt and record everything we find to test our hypotheses.

First, we conduct a survey, which is where archaeologists walk around a site looking for evidence of ancient populations on the surface. This evidence can include pottery, tools, and even buildings. There is a higher chance of finding something beneath the surface wherever we discover a greater number of surface finds!

After we choose where to dig, we plan the details of the excavation, like how long we will excavate or if we will excavate small **pits** or in an **open context**. Then, the digging begins! At the end of the excavation, we can see the unique order of construction and destruction events that happened at that site.

8   Excavation pit and baulk

So how does an excavation work?

It's kind of like eating a layered cake, and it relates to the Earth's geologic processes. Imagine you are making a delicious cake with four layers. Which layer do you make first? That's right – the bottom layer! Then you add some frosting and maybe some sprinkles, then you add the next layer, and continue the process until you finish the cake! You build the cake from the bottom-up.

The Earth's geology and layers of human occupation at a site work in the same way! Over millions of years, changing environmental conditions cause different layers of rock and dirt to build upon one another. Over time, we end up with what geologists (earth scientists) call a stratigraphic sequence, or a series of rock layers.

The oldest layer is found at the bottom of the sequence, while the youngest layer is found at the surface. Each layer tells geologists what the environment was like when it formed. Sites where people have lived over hundreds or thousands of years build in the same way, with the oldest layers of occupation at the bottom of a sequence, and the most recent occupation level at the top.

Each layer of different colored dirt shows a different period of time!

Now imagine that you are ready to eat that cake! How do you cut it? From the top down, right? When we excavate, that is exactly what we are doing! Cutting a slice of time through a site from top to bottom, with the most recent events found at the top, and the oldest events at the bottom.

When you cut out a slice of cake, you can see the whole thing from the inside-out. You see each layer of cake, frosting, and sprinkles you added to build it. You can see the cake's stratigraphy, or the layers that make it up.

The same goes for excavations when we dig at a site! Archaeologists excavate from the top down, and are looking at the stratigraphy of a site to understand the order of events that happened while people lived there.

We can tell construction events from destruction events (such as a fire that destroys a part of a site). We can see in the stratigraphy when a site was abandoned, and we can even see when someone who lived at the site more recently dug into older layers to build a trash pit or a wall foundation! Everything we find inside each stratum, or layer, helps archaeologists understand who lived at that site and what activities they participated in.

Archaeologists dig each stratum very carefully, taking note of the color and consistency of the dirt, along with what types of artifacts are found inside the **context**. We collect samples of the dirt layers to test for things such as seeds to tell what plants were growing or food was being eaten. We also collect **pottery sherds**, **lithic** (or stone) tools, and a large variety of other artifacts and samples which help us to fully understand the activities and age of a site.

We record the location where each sample or artifact was found, both **vertically** and **horizontally** in space, to map them and understand how each artifact relates to the others during our later analysis of the site.

Ideally, the excavation continues down until we reach either the **bedrock** or soil layer under the first layer of occupation. In this way, archaeologists get a general understanding of the different people who occupied a site from the first people who lived there until the most recent. Some sites are occupied only for a few decades or centuries, while others, like Rome in Italy or London in the United Kingdom, have had people living there **continuously** for thousands of years! Imagine all of the different groups of people who have lived in those places over time!

Gobekli Tepe, Turkey

Palace of Knossos, Crete

Pompeii, Italy

Remember that cake? What happens when you have finished eating it? That's right, it is gone forever! The same thing happens during an excavation.

Archaeologists are very careful to make sure that they record as much information as possible, because once something is dug out of the ground, it can never go back, and any information about its context is lost! We want to make sure future archaeologists can access as much information as possible about the sites we dig, so we record all kinds of information: measurements, stratigraphic drawings, the color of each dirt layer we encounter.

And once we collect all of this information from a site, whether it is a bunch of tiny pits or the excavation of an entire area, the data is analyzed and published for anyone to read about later. This is the most important thing archaeologists can do for future archaeologists!

13

Do you think archaeologists have always excavated in such detail?

No! Archaeology has developed over the last 150 years to be the scientific field that it is today! The earliest archaeologists were more like movie treasure hunters—they dug through as much dirt as possible to find exciting artifacts like gold masks and giant statues! And they found some amazing things, too, like the lost city of Troy, ancient Mesopotamian palaces, and priceless Egyptian sculptures!

However, they also lost a lot of valuable information through their destructive practices, like several layers of occupation in the city of Troy, which were lost when Heinrich Schliemann plowed through them to get to the Troy of Homer's Iliad.

Archaeologists have learned from both the successes and mistakes of past archaeologists to create the discipline of archaeology we know today.

Ruins of Troy, Turkey

Archaeology is all about answering the question "how did past people live?"

Have you ever wondered what a Neanderthal in Spain ate for dinner? An archaeologist can tell you that! We take samples of dirt or use animal bones with teeth marks to figure it out!

How did the Egyptians build the pyramids? Well, now we know that they probably poured water in front of the stones as they pulled them to create less friction against the ground. That made it easier to move the gigantic stones up a smooth sand ramp to the tops of the pyramids!

What did ancient houses look like? In areas in the Middle East, archaeologists find the remains of mudbrick houses; in other areas, people built their homes out of wood; all over the world, we have found that many humans spent time in caves for shelter.

Some people lived in giant cities, like Cahokia, found today in Missouri, or Nineveh in modern Mosul. Others lived in small communities like the families living at Must Farm in England, or in **hunter-gatherer** groups, like many aboriginal people in Australia.

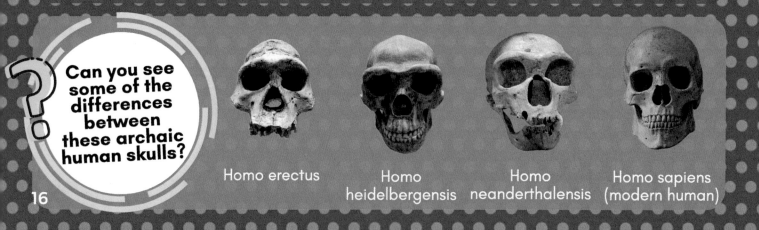

Can you see some of the differences between these archaic human skulls?

Homo erectus

Homo heidelbergensis

Homo neanderthalensis

Homo sapiens (modern human)

Pyramids at Giza, Egypt

Stonehenge, United Kingdom

Cahokia Mounds, United States

How did people get the materials they needed for tools and housing?

Trade has always been an important part of most human societies, and archaeologists are often able to trace the extent of trade routes by recording where specific artifact types, raw materials, or food seeds have been found.

For example, archaeologists know that precious blue rocks called lapis lazuli were traded from Afghanistan to Egypt, beginning around 5000 years ago! We know this because lapis lazuli is a rare stone found only in specific locations naturally, so when it shows up hundreds and thousands of miles away, we know people must have taken it there.

Another material we can easily trace is obsidian, which is a black volcanic glass that makes excellent blades. Obsidian is found only near volcanoes, so obsidian blades found in non-volcanic areas also shows the movement of people and materials.

By tracing the movement of artifacts, technology, and ancient seeds, archaeologists get a better understanding of the movements and interactions of ancient people.

The earliest writing systems were used to record trade and other economic interactions on clay tablets!

Large libraries of detailed transaction records (like a credit card statement) were preserved when the buildings housing them burned down. These records show the importance of keeping track of what goods came from where on a daily basis.

THE MAKING OF
King Tutankhamun's Golden Mask

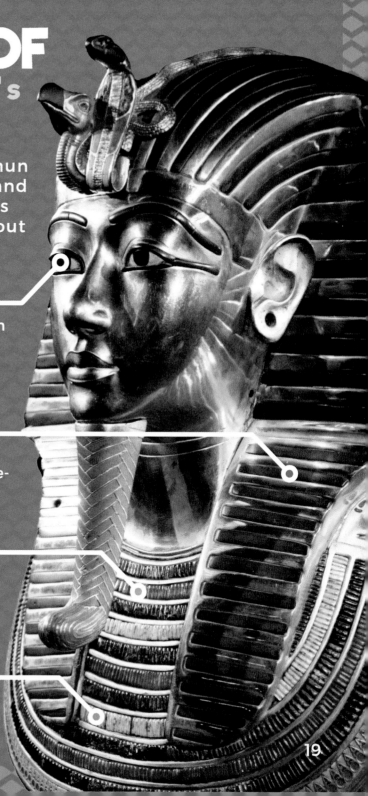

The golden mask of King Tutankhamun highlights the importance of trade and shows the long distances materials moved during the time he lived (about 1341-1323 BCE).

Obsidian was imported from the Mediterranean and was used here to create the pupils of his eyes.

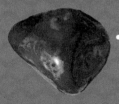

Lapis lazuli was brought from Afganistan and represented life-giving water and the sky.

Carnelian was important because It represented the sun.

Turquoise represented the goddess Hathor, and came from mines in Sinai.

Roman Forum, Italy

How do archaeologists learn so much about people who no longer live?

We study the things we find in the ground that were left there long ago. When people live somewhere, their activities leave traces behind. This could be parts of the walls from collapsed houses, bones of the people which are often left in some sort of grave, or items of daily use that manage to be preserved through time like pots and pans or arrow heads.

Native American burial mound, United States 21

Mortuary Temple of Rameses along the line of cultivation along the Nile River

Example of ancient mudbrick construction, Deir el–Hagar, Egypt

Remains of a Bronze Age settlement at Must Farm, United Kingdom

Structural remains can be clearly defined, or they can be difficult to detect. Temples and palaces in Egypt are often easy to detect for several reasons. They are typically found on the edges of the desert, where few people can live, so the ancient buildings have never been built over by later generations of Egyptians. Also, they are constructed out of materials, such as limestone, that endure in the dry conditions of the desert.

Ancient Egyptians constructed their houses out of mudbrick, which is dried mud that easily breaks down when it gets wet. Between the movement of the Nile River across its bed and people living in the same locations for thousands of years, it is very difficult to find their ancient homes, while we easily find the remains of the stone palaces.

Several cultures across North America and northern Europe built their homes out of material such as wood, which degrades over time, leaving behind only traces of the structures ever having been there. When looking for these types of homes, archaeologists look for **stains** in the dirt from where organic material breaks down differently than the surrounding dirt, which leaves behind different colored dirt.

Whether a site has well-preserved foundations and walls or has buildings recognized through stains, archaeologists use these as references to create a site plan, which allows us to understand the whole site rather than just individual structures.

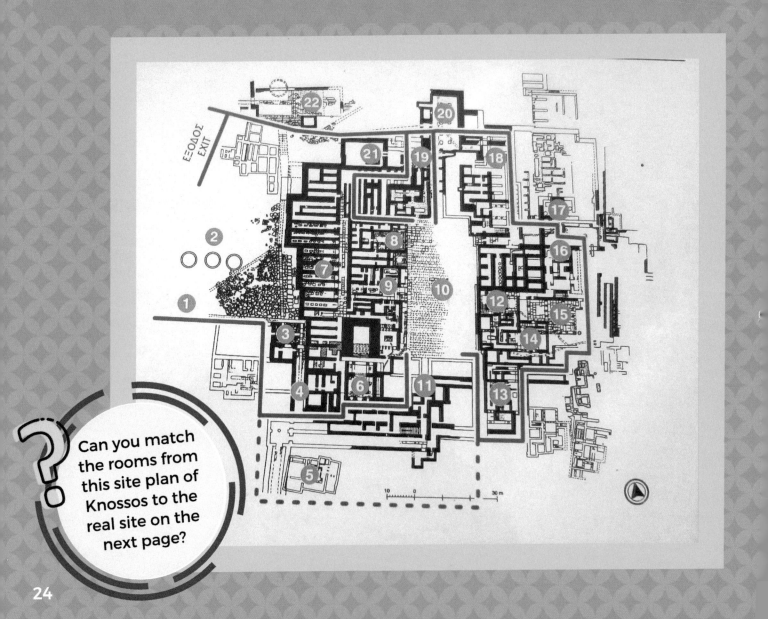

Can you match the rooms from this site plan of Knossos to the real site on the next page?

Knossos
Κνωσός

Minos

25

Archaeologists also learn a lot about past people by studying their bones. We can tell what types of food they ate regularly through isotope analysis, which identifies the elements that are present in the bones, especially in teeth. Bones can also tell us what type of lifestyle someone led.

Have you ever broken a bone? Doctors today take x-rays to look at your bones and can see injuries that happened in the past. Trained archaeologists can look carefully at ancient bones and tell what kind of injuries a person got while living, as well as whether he or she suffered from certain diseases. This allows us to understand how that person lived, and sometimes how they died.

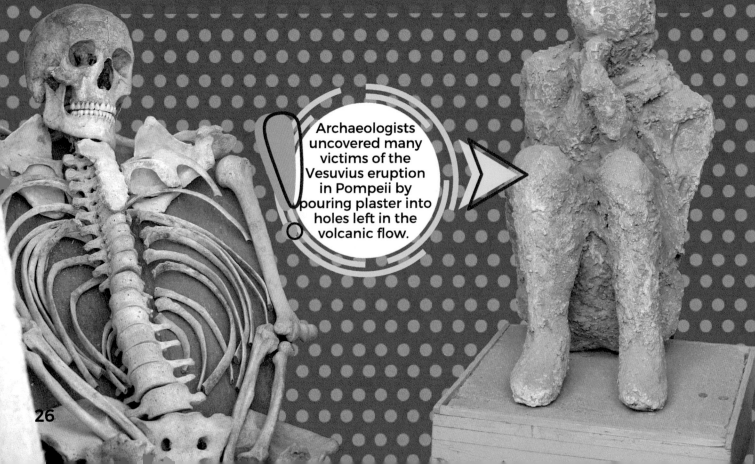

Archaeologists uncovered many victims of the Vesuvius eruption in Pompeii by pouring plaster into holes left in the volcanic flow.

Taj Mahal, India

Poulnabrone Dolmen, Ireland

Egyptian Sarcophagus

Terra Cotta Army, China

Human remains can also tell us about the culture a person lived in:

Were they buried in a ritual manner or left in the wild? Were they buried with items of wealth? What did the people who loved the deceased find important to take with them after they died? The answers to these questions give us great insight into how societies viewed death, and sometimes, an afterlife.

27

When we excavate, archaeologists also find items that people used while they were living. Take a moment to think about some of the things you have at home that you use every day: dishes, clothes, brushes, tables and chairs, stoves and ovens, bathrooms, pencils, cars and bicycles, books, computers, and many other things!

Someday, many years from now, future archaeologists may be excavating your house to see how you lived, and what would they find? That's right – many of the things you use every day! And that is exactly what archaeologists find when they excavate ancient homes.

We find pots, pans, and bowls from the kitchen; ancient tablets that are like the books you read; remains of carts and horses for travelling; sometimes even leftover dinner. We regularly find art projects, tools, and even board games!

Bread from Pompeii

Amphorae

Sumerian tablets

So how can you get involved in archaeology today?

There are so many different ways you can get involved, from reading more about archaeology to visiting a museum with unique artifacts to joining an excavation near you! I started by reading everything I could get my hands on about history and archaeology and different cultures: books, magazines, and news articles. These are all easy to find online and in libraries.

Another way to learn more about archaeology is to go to a museum near your home or visit one when your family is traveling. Museums are one of the best places to learn about the history of where you are, and there are more museums out there than you might imagine! Visit museums big and small to see actual artifacts excavated by archaeologists around the world!

You can also join an excavation near you! Community archaeology is one of the most exciting trends in archaeology right now, where archaeologists either ask the local community to come out and learn how to excavate at a local site or just show off everything they are learning about what happened in the past where you live. It is one of the best ways to dig up the history around you!

And don't forget International Archaeology Day, which is held on the third Saturday of October. Many archaeological organizations invite guests of all ages to participate in archaeology-related activities across the globe. Make sure you find some fun archaeology near you!

Excavations in Rome, Italy

Great Wall of China

As you can see, there are MANY different ways to study our human past! We have learned that archaeology is the study of the human past through the excavation of sites where people lived and that archaeologists are the scientists who study archaeology. We learned about the process of excavation and about some of the things archaeologists find at a site. We also learned some of the different ways that scientists learn the details about the history of a site.

What would you study if you were an archaeologist? Why?

What is the most important thing an archaeologist should do when excavating?

If an archaeologist were to excavate your bedroom, what would they learn about you?

How can archaeology change the way we understand the past?

I hope you have enjoyed this book!

If you did, I would REALLY appreciate you leaving a review on Amazon!

Connect with Me:
On Facebook @pandaarchaeology
On Instagram @panda_archaeology

ABOUT THE AUTHOR

Amanda is an archaeologist, educator, and enthusiast of all things related to past cultures. Her mission is to encourage children to have a passion for learning and exploring the world around them!

She has over ten years of experience working with children of all ages, and earned her BA in Anthropology and Mediterranean Archaeology from Emory University and her MPhil in Archaeology from the University of Cambridge.

When she is not writing, you can find Amanda planning her next excavation adventure, staring out at the stars, reading something from either Douglas Adams, Mark Twain, or J.R.R. Tolkien, or coming to the conclusion that, once again, there is always next year for the Atlanta Braves.

At Panda Archaeology, we provide tools and resources for children, teachers, and parents to become engaged in the history that is all around them and throughout the world!

Images

Made in the USA
Monee, IL
22 January 2021